Immigrating to America

Michelle R. Prather, M.A.

Consultant

Jennifer M. Lopez, NBCT, M.S.Ed.
Teacher Specialist—History/Social Studies
Office of Curriculum & Instruction
Norfolk Public Schools

Publishing Credits

Rachelle Cracchiolo, M.S.Ed., *Publisher*
Emily R. Smith, M.A.Ed., *VP of Content Development*
Véronique Bos, *Creative Director*
Robin Erickson, *Art Director*

Image Credits: front cover, p.1, p.6 (right), p.11 (left), p.15 (middle) Everett Historical/Shutterstock; pp.2–3 Library of Congress [LC-USZ62-38214]; p.4 Library of Congress [LC-DIG-stereo-1s08151]; p.5 (left) Joe Raedle/Getty Images; p.7, p.9 (left) SSPL/Getty Images; p.8 Granger; p.9 (right) Zeno. org; p.10, p.23, p.25 (bottom), p.27 (top) U.S. National Archives; p.11 (right) Library of Congress [LC-USZC2-780]; p.12 Corbis via Getty Images; p.13 (top) Boulder County Latino History; p.13 (bottom) Library of Congress [LC-USF34-009869-C]; p.14, p.15 (top, bottom), p.16, p.19 New York Public Library; p.17 (top) South Asian American Digital Archive; p.17 (bottom) Library of Congress [LC-USZ62-22339]; p.18 BnF Gallica; p.20 (insert) Library of Congress [LC-USZ62-86667]; pp.20–21 Santa Barbara Museum of Art; p.21 (top) Sean O'Neill via Flickr; p.22 (left) Simon Allardice via Flickr; p.22 (right) National Library of Medicine; p.24 Library of Congress [LC-DIG-highsm-25218]; p.25 (top) Bettmann/Getty Images; p.26 Joseph Sohm/Shutterstock; p.27 (bottom) Maryland State Archives; p.28 Library of Congress [LC-DIG-ppmsca-51996]; p.29 National Park Service, Statue of Liberty NM; p.31 Library of Congress [LC-USF34-018215-E]; p.32 krblokhin/iStock; all other images from iStock and/ or Shutterstock.

Library of Congress Cataloging-in-Publication Data

Names: Prather, Michelle Renee, 1975- author.
Title: Immigrating to America / Michelle R. Prather, M.A.
Description: Huntington Beach : Teacher Created Materials, 2022. | Audience: Grades K-1 (provided by Teacher Created Materials) | Description based on print version record and CIP data provided by publisher; resource not viewed.
Identifiers: LCCN 2020006606 (print) | LCCN 2020006607 (ebook) | ISBN 9781425834432 (ebook) | ISBN 9781425850630 (paperback) | ISBN 9781425850630q(paperback) | ISBN 9781425834432q(ebook)
Subjects: LCSH: Immigrants--United States--History--Juvenile literature. | United States--Emigration and immigration--Juvenile literature.
Classification: LCC JV6450 (ebook) | LCC JV6450 .P73 2020 (print) | DDC 304.8/73--dc23
LC record available at https://lccn.loc.gov/2020006606

Teacher Created Materials

5482 Argosy Drive
Huntington Beach, CA 92649
www.tcmpub.com

ISBN 978-1-4258-5063-0

© 2022 Teacher Created Materials, Inc.

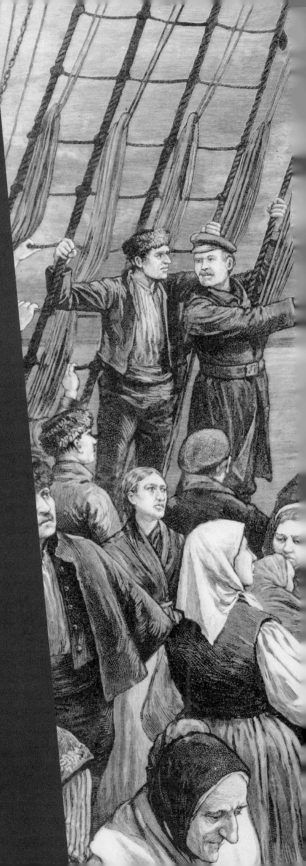

Table of Contents

A New World

> "It was very disrupting…to pack and break up your home. Oh, we took…clothing and some pieces of china…a blanket or two also that were real good wool, that we felt maybe we may not be able to get here in the United States."
> —Emma Greiner

It was 1925. Eleven-year-old Emma Greiner and her twelve-year-old brother, William, traveled to the United States from Italy. Their father had **immigrated** about five years earlier, and he missed them a lot. Emma and William had their aunts and each other. But they were about to leave behind a lifetime of memories.

▲ Early twentieth-century immigrants wait to enter the United States.

4

For hundreds of years, people from around the world have done just that. They have moved to the United States seeking freedom and better lives. The risks can be great, and the journey can be difficult. Success isn't guaranteed. But people still hope for better lives when they make the brave and life-changing move.

The early twentieth century saw a flood of immigration to the United States. Between 1880 and 1930, more than 27 million people made the tough journey. These people shaped the country's languages, traditions, politics, and **economy**. If they had not made the United States their home, the country would look very different today. Those people changed the United States forever.

 A group of modern-day immigrants become U.S. citizens.

What's the Difference?

The terms *emigrant* and *immigrant* are not the same. The term *emigrant* is used to describe someone who moves *away* from a country. For example, people can emigrate from the United States to other countries. The term *immigrant* is used to describe someone who moves *to* a new country, such as a person immigrating to the United States from a different country. Both terms have *migrant* as their base, which means "one who moves."

A Changing Nation

A Global Empire

The Russian Empire existed for nearly two hundred years. It was absolutely massive. The empire covered about one-sixth of all land on Earth. At its peak, the Russian Empire covered much of Europe, Asia, and even part of North America. The empire finally broke up in 1917.

Changing Laws

In 1921, the U.S. government passed the Emergency Quota Act. This act set quotas, or limits, on the number of immigrants allowed into the country each year. This law was a response to the increasing number of new immigrants, specifically Jewish immigrants. Their quotas were much lower than those of other immigrant groups. This racist law stayed in place until 1965.

Most early twentieth-century immigrants to the East Coast were from southern and eastern European countries. In earlier years, most people had come from countries in western and northern Europe, such as Ireland and Germany. Now, millions of people moved from places like Italy and the Russian Empire. These people were called "new immigrants." This term came into use because their **cultures** were very different from people who had come before. Many new immigrants were Catholic or Jewish. Most of them did not speak English well. **Nativists** were afraid this group of people would harm their way of life because their cultures were so different.

New immigrants had faced problems at home. In Italy, the gap between the rich and the poor was growing. The people living

▼ **a Jewish immigrant in 1911**

in the Russian Empire faced **starvation**. At the same time, the Second Industrial Revolution was beginning in the United States. This was a time of extreme economic growth. Factory owners were hiring workers as quickly as they could. For people who were facing hunger at home, these jobs seemed like a dream. Stories about the United States made it sound almost perfect.

Most immigrants settled in cities. That is where the majority of jobs were located. Big cities, such as New York, Chicago, and Philadelphia, grew quickly. Soon, these places became too crowded. They could not support the amount of people moving in.

▼ Workers bottle ketchup at a New York City factory in 1910.

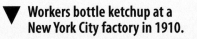

The New East Coast

As more and more immigrants settled in cities on the East Coast, transportation became a major issue. Immigrants found work building bridges. They helped build streetcar lines and subways. Millions of immigrants helped build the railroad system. Then, they worked to keep it running.

Housing was also a challenge. Cities were unprepared for the millions of new residents. Construction quickly began on **tenement** buildings. These structures were quick and cheap to build. They were usually four to six stories tall. The apartments inside were very small (about the same size as two parking spaces). In that tiny space, there was a bedroom, a kitchen, and a front room. Families—mostly immigrants—packed into these tight spaces. A magazine at the time referred to these buildings as "death-traps." An architect said they were "the worst curse which ever **afflicted** any great community." By the turn of the century, most people in New York City were living in tenements.

Even with these problems, people still came. Between 1900 and 1929, more than 15 million people emigrated from Europe to the United States!

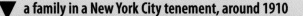 a family in a New York City tenement, around 1910

Powerful Photos

In 1888, Jacob Riis took photos (like the one above) of homeless children and dirty tenements. These photos became famous. Because of them, people demanded better laws for immigrants. Riis had a personal interest in the subject—he was an immigrant. He had a much different life from the people he was photographing, though. Riis was a very close friend of President Theodore Roosevelt.

A Changing Landscape

By 1900, New York City was a mix of cultures. It had more Irish residents than Dublin, Ireland. Only Rome, Italy, had more Italian residents. More Jewish people lived in New York City than in any other city in the world. Ten years later, three-fourths of the people in New York City were immigrants or the children of immigrants.

▲ More than half of the workers who built the Empire State Building were immigrants.

The New West Coast

At the turn of the twentieth century, seventy percent of immigrants entered the United States through New York City. Even so, the West Coast and the Southwest were handling hundreds of thousands of new arrivals. Most of these people were coming from Asia and Mexico. In particular, Chinese immigrants came in huge numbers.

Chinese people had lived on the West Coast since the gold rush. Years later, Chinese workers played a critical role in building railroad lines. When the U.S. economy was doing well, Chinese people were

"Paper Families"

There were a few **exceptions** to the Chinese Exclusion Act. People with special skills could still come to the United States. People with fathers who were U.S. citizens could also come. This led some Chinese immigrants to join "paper families." These people bought fake paperwork that said their fathers were U.S. citizens. They had to memorize details on the papers. Then, immigrants had to pass interviews about their fake families.

The Citrus Wizard

When Lue Gim Gong was 12 years old, he moved from China to the United States. He lived in San Francisco for a few years before moving to Florida. Florida suffered a few harsh winters and many orange crops were lost. Lue wanted to help. He bred new types of oranges, apples, tomatoes, grapefruit, and peaches that were more likely to survive cold winters. Lue's work helped the nation.

▲ paperwork for a Chinese immigrant from 1910

treated fairly. But in the 1870s, the economy struggled. People in the West blamed immigrants for taking their jobs. Americans pressured the government to act.

In 1882, Congress passed a new law. It was called the Chinese Exclusion Act. This act **banned** Chinese workers from entering the United States. It also affected Chinese people already in the United States. If they left the country, they had to be approved to reenter. This was the first time a federal law shut out people due to their **nationality**. This act slowed immigration from China for the next century.

◀ This 1886 cartoon supports the Chinese Exclusion Act.

▼ This 1882 cartoon criticizes the Chinese Exclusion Act.

In the 1920s, the U.S. economy was booming. Workers were needed in the Southwest to help on farms, in mines, and in construction. Chinese immigration, though, had nearly stopped. Thousands of people left Mexico and moved north to find work. U.S. business owners welcomed them. Like most other immigrants, Mexican **laborers** were paid less than white American workers.

In 1929, the Great Depression began. Millions of people lost their jobs. Once again, people blamed immigrants. More than two million Mexicans and Mexican Americans left the United States over the next seven years. Half of those people were U.S. citizens.

Then, the United States joined World War II in 1941. It was clear that American farmers would not have enough workers for their farms. So the U.S. government encouraged Mexican farm workers to come once more. More than four million Mexicans and Mexican Americans moved to the United States during the war.

▲ A family from Mexico travels to work on U.S. farms in 1944.

Even though Mexicans had come to help, the workers were treated poorly. They worked long hours. They were paid around 30 cents per hour (around $4 per hour in today's money). After the war, U.S. farmers had come to depend on their labor. The work program stayed in place until 1964. Then, the U.S. government **deported** more than one million people to Mexico.

Mexican Families Being Deported At County's Expense

Another group of Mexican families will be provided transportation out of Boulder county, and will depart Saturday, Mrs. Florence Burton, county welfare worker, said today. The county is paying their traveling expenses as far as El Paso. Yesterday, four families were given transportation.

The Mexicans came to this county in hope of getting work as beet field laborers, it was said.

Many Starving

Leaving the United States

There was no law that forced people to leave in 1929. But they were strongly encouraged to do so. Government officials handed out tickets for trains going to Mexico and told people they would be "better off" leaving. This removal is widely believed to have made the Great Depression much worse than it would have otherwise been.

Fighting on Two Fronts

Hundreds of thousands of Mexicans and Mexican Americans joined the U.S. armed forces during World War II. One of those soldiers was Armando Flores. One day, Flores was standing with his hands in his pockets. "American soldiers stand at attention," a lieutenant told him. That moment stuck with Flores for years. "Nobody had ever called me an American before!" he later said.

The Ellis Island Experience

Meeting Moore

Workers at Ellis Island processed their first immigrants on New Year's Day in 1892. A steamship unloaded 124 passengers from Europe. Among these passengers was Annie Moore. Moore was 17 years old and from Ireland. She had made the trip with her two younger brothers and would be meeting their parents in New York. After 12 days at sea, Moore was the first immigrant to be processed at Ellis Island.

Finding Fame

Many immigrants who passed through Ellis Island would go on to find fame in the United States. Bob Hope moved from England to become a famous actor and theater star. Irving Berlin left the Russian Empire and wrote "God Bless America." Albert Einstein moved from Germany and became a famous scientist. Even the Italian man Ettore Boiardi (better known as "Chef Boyardee") passed through Ellis Island!

With millions of immigrants arriving in the United States, it became clear that there needed to be a system in place. Before the 1870s, entering the United States was fairly easy. Each state made its own rules about who could enter. Some states had strict laws. Other states had no laws at all. This process stayed confusing and unorganized until 1875. That was when the **Supreme Court** ruled that the U.S. government should be in charge of all immigration into the country.

One of the first things the government did was build immigration stations. These stations helped the government keep track of who was coming into the country. Workers checked immigrants' health and legal histories. If people failed these exams, they could be **detained** or sent back to their home countries.

More than 70 stations were built along the shores of the United States. The largest and busiest of these stations was Ellis Island in New York. Ellis Island opened in 1892. This turned out to be important timing. Millions of immigrants from Europe would soon arrive to find work during the Second Industrial Revolution.

▼ Ellis Island immigrants wait to be examined.

Although the Ellis Island experience seemed intense to immigrants, the process could be fairly quick. First, the ship docked near Staten Island. There, doctors would board the ship and check for dangerous diseases.

Once doctors confirmed the ship was clean, immigration officers boarded and asked questions. Officers interviewed passengers by **class**. First- and second-class passengers went first. Third-class passengers were last and had to have their bags checked for illegal goods.

When officers were satisfied with passengers' answers, they were placed on smaller boats and taken to Ellis Island. Once they arrived, passengers were sorted into two lines. One line was for women and children. The other line was for men and boys over 16 years old.

When passengers reached the front of the line, doctors examined them. People who passed the exam were sent forward. Next, immigration officers asked more detailed questions. If the officers did not believe passengers' answers, they were detained. If officers approved of passengers' answers, they could enter the country. Most immigrants passed through Ellis Island in around two to three hours.

▼ Inspection cards showed that immigrants had passed health exams during the trip.

Chalk Check

If passengers did not pass the medical exam, their clothes were marked with chalk letters. For example, the letter *B* stood for back problems and *H* stood for heart problems. Then, people were sent to the "doctor's pen." About 1 in 10 passengers were sent to the doctor's pen. There, they waited for more thorough checks, which could take days or weeks to complete.

Getting the Job Done

World War I began in 1914. The United States joined the war three years later. New immigrants played a critical role in the war effort. About one in six U.S. soldiers was born outside the United States. On the home front, immigrants kept businesses running. One-third of the workers at the nation's largest steel company were immigrants.

 Ellis Island doctors examine new arrivals.

A Symbol of Hope

Nearly 14 million immigrants entered the country through Ellis Island between 1886 and 1924. They came to escape religious **persecution**, to find work, and for other reasons.

One of the first things people saw when they arrived in New York was the Statue of Liberty. The sight of it was a relief. It seemed to say, "You are welcome here. You are safe." It became an important symbol of the United States.

The Statue of Liberty was a gift from France. The countries were **allies** during the American Revolution. The statue honored that friendship. It also symbolized the freedom that the United States offered. To many people, the United States promised independence. The statue was a symbol of that promise.

The Statue of Liberty was first proposed in 1865. The creators wanted their statue to have a meaningful name. So, they called it Liberty **Enlightening** the World. The name reflects the importance of freedom.

In 1871, Liberty's designer traveled to the United States to find a place to put the statue. He decided on Bedloe's Island. People on ships entering New York would have a clear view of the island. He knew placing the statue there would help welcome newcomers.

Édouard's Idea

Édouard de Laboulaye (eh-DWAR duh la-boo-LAY) was a French **scholar**. He came up with the idea for the statue. He wanted the people, not a king, to lead France. However, he did not want violence. So de Laboulaye chose sculptor Frédéric-Auguste Bartholdi (freh-deh-REEK oh-GOOST bar-TOLL-dee) to direct the design. De Laboulaye hoped the statue would inspire peaceful change.

A Breath of Fresh Air

"One day, the captain announced that we were entering the harbor of New York City, and that there was a marvelous statue there that would greet us. And they invited us to come up to the decks. So that was one of the happiest days of my life."
—Emma Greiner

construction on the Statue of Liberty in 1883 in Paris, France

In June 1885, the statue was shipped from France in pieces. When it arrived in the United States, there was a big problem—the **pedestal** was not ready yet! Congress had set aside money to build the pedestal. However, the project had cost too much and had run out of funding. French and U.S. celebrities asked people to donate money to help pay for the pedestal. For $1 donations, people received 6-inch (15-centimeter) model statues. For $5 donations, they received 12-inch (30-centimeter) statues. Joseph Pulitzer also offered to print all donors' names in his newspapers.

For a year after its arrival, the statue sat in **crates** on Bedloe's Island. Then, it was built, piece by piece. On

Statue of "Liberty Enlightening the World."

The Committee in charge of the construction of the base and pedestal for the reception of this great work, **in order to raise funds for its completion,** have prepared a miniature Statuette *six inches in height*—the Statue Bronzed; Pedestal, Nickel-silvered—which they are now delivering to subscribers throughout the United States at **One Dollar Each.**

This attractive souvenir and Mantel or Desk ornament is a *perfect fac-simile* of the model furnished by the artist.

The Statuette in same metal, *twelve inches high*, at **Five Dollars Each,** delivered.

The designs of Statue and Pedestal are protected by U. S. Patents, and the models can *only* be furnished by this Committee. Address, with remittance,

RICHARD BUTLER, Secretary,

American Committee of the Statue of Liberty,

33 Mercer Street, New York.

▼ People in Paris pay to view a model of the statue's arm in 1884.

October 28, 1886, the statue was revealed. One million people made the trip to see the presentation in person.

The statue's details make it clear that it is for all people. She holds a tablet in her left hand that reads "JULY IV MDCCLXXVI" (July 4, 1776, in Roman numerals). That is the date the United States declared its independence. At the statue's feet, there are broken chains to show the end of **oppression**. And she wears a crown with seven rays—one for each continent.

"The New Colossus"

One of the most famous details of the statue is its poem. It was written by Emma Lazarus as part of the fundraising effort for the pedestal. The most famous lines are:

"Give me your tired, your poor, Your huddled masses yearning to breathe free."

Lazarus died in 1887, and over the years, the poem was forgotten by many people. In 1901, one of Lazarus's friends began working to have the poem added to the statue. Two years later, her efforts paid off, and the poem was added to a plaque on the statue's pedestal.

The Angel Island Experience

Being Detained

At Ellis Island, most immigrants made it into the country in a few hours. If they were detained, it was usually for a few days or weeks at the most. At Angel Island, the average time people were detained was around six months. Some immigrants were kept on the island for nearly two years.

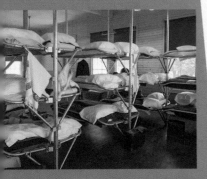

Ellis Island was the entry point for most immigrants who came from northern and western Europe. On the other side of the United States was Angel Island. When it opened in San Francisco in 1910, this station was referred to as the "Ellis Island of the West."

Angel Island was the entry point for immigrants from more than 80 countries. Most people came from China. Other large groups of immigrants also came from Japan, eastern Russia, and India. No one knows the total number of people who were held or passed through the immigration station. Historians think it could be as high as one million people.

Protest It!

The conditions for people who were detained on Angel Island were cramped and dirty. Rooms that were built to house no more than 60 people were often packed with 200 people. Members of the Chinese government even had to step in. They asked Chinese shops in San Francisco to **boycott** American goods until the center was improved.

▲ A charity worker sits with detained Chinese immigrants in 1923.

Immigration officers interview a man from China.

Some Ellis Island immigrants were detained. However, 98 percent of immigrants at Ellis Island were allowed to enter the country. Things were different at Angel Island. The station was a way to enforce the Chinese Exclusion Act. So, the process was very strict. Immigrants at Angel Island faced much more **discrimination**.

Angel Island was designed to make immigrants feel isolated, or alone. The station was on an island by itself. There was no Statue of Liberty to offer hope and comfort. Instead, immigrants were kept apart—scared and nervous.

Imprisoned in the Wood Building

Like at Ellis Island, the immigration process at Angel Island began on ships. Doctors and officers separated people into two groups based on their nationalities. First-class passengers and people from eastern Europe were put in one group. This group was often given immediate access to the country. The rest of the ships' passengers were put in another group. This group mainly consisted of people from Asia.

This second group was taken to Angel Island. They had to give specific details about their lives. Angel Island officials wanted to be sure that immigrants were not claiming to be people they were not. Family members in the United States also had to answer questions. The whole family could be deported if their answers did not match. It was intense and scary.

While immigrants waited to hear whether they could stay in the country, they were kept on the island. Some immigrants dealt with their feelings by carving words into the immigration station walls. There are poems that express fears. Other carvings describe not being able to sleep. Today, these carvings are a powerful sign of the fear and loneliness that many immigrants felt.

wall carvings at Angel Island ▶

▲ Officers inspect passports of Japanese immigrants in 1920.

▼ Immigrants from Asia arrive at Angel Island.

The Island Today

Angel Island is now a museum. The Angel Island Immigration Station Foundation provides public tours of the grounds. People can see where immigrants slept and view hundreds of wall carvings. The foundation says it hopes people view the island as "a place for reflection and discovery of our shared history as a nation of immigrants."

Q & A

These are a few of the questions Jung Joong, a 19-year-old Chinese immigrant, had to answer. Officials drew a map of his village based on his answers, and his father's answers had to match the map perfectly. In total, Jung Joong answered over 170 questions.

Q: *How many rows of houses are there in the village?*
A: five rows

Q: *In which row is your house located?*
A: third house second row; counting from the north

Q: *How many houses are in the first row?*
A: four, including the school

An American Success Story

James Truslow Adams was a successful businessman before becoming a writer and scholar. He was born in Brooklyn, New York. Like most Americans, though, Adams had an immigrant history. His father was born in Venezuela. He saw firsthand how people's lives could change when they moved to the United States.

Washington's Wish

In 1788, George Washington wrote a letter to a Dutch leader. In it, Washington expressed his dreams for the future of the United States. He said he hoped the new nation would be a "safe & agreeable **asylum**." He said this sense of safety should belong to all people, regardless of "whatever nation they might belong" to.

The Real American Dream

The "American Dream" brings to mind all the things people in the United States can have if they work hard. The phrase was not intended only for people born in the United States. James Truslow Adams first used the term in his book *The Epic of America* in 1931. He wrote that the American Dream is a hope that "life should be better and richer and fuller for everyone." He continued that the American Dream was for everyone, regardless of "birth or position."

Early immigrants came to the United States with that same sense of hope. They wanted the freedom to build a bright future. They wanted to live in places where their races or religions did not stop them from reaching their goals. They were not always treated fairly. But they worked hard to leave their mark on the United States.

The hopes of immigrants today are no different. They want to lead better lives. For many people, the United States gives them a chance to do just that. It gives them a chance to see their very own American Dream realized.

Analyze It!

The Statue of Liberty quickly became a symbol of the United States. It signified freedom and hope. Americans and immigrants alike were inspired by Lady Liberty.

The image below appeared in *Frank Leslie's Illustrated Newspaper* in July 1887. It was printed nine months after the statue was unveiled. The people in the drawing are third-class passengers.

[JULY 9, 1887.   325

FRANK LESLIE'S ILLUSTRATED NEWSPAPER.

NEW YORK.—WELCOME TO THE LAND OF FREEDOM—AN OCEAN STEAMER PASSING THE STATUE OF LIBERTY: SCENE ON THE STEERAGE DECK

The image below was on the cover of *Judge* magazine in 1890. It was drawn as a response to the Secretary of the Treasury William Windom. Windom wanted to build an immigration station on Bedloe's Island, where the Statue of Liberty was. (The station was later built on Ellis Island.)

Compare and contrast the two images.

How do the titles indicate the artists' purposes?

Look closely at the details of the artwork. What does each image say about immigration?

How are immigrants shown?

How does each artist show Lady Liberty?

THE PROPOSED EMIGRANT DUMPING SITE.

STATUE OF LIBERTY—"Mr. Windom, if you are going to make this island a garbage heap, I am going back to France."

Glossary

afflicted—caused someone or something pain or suffering

allies—people who join together for a common cause or goal

asylum—a place of shelter and safety

banned—stopped from doing something

boycott—to refuse to work with a country, organization, or person to express disapproval and to force them to accept terms

class—one of the sections of seats or beds on an airplane, train, ship, etc.

crates—large boxes used for moving things from one place to another

cultures—the customs, beliefs, and ways of life of groups or societies

deported—forced people who are not citizens of countries to leave

detained—held or kept at a place

discrimination—unfair treatment of a person or group

economy—the system by which goods and services are made, sold, and bought

enlightening—giving knowledge

exceptions—instances where rules do not apply

immigrated—came to a country or place to live

laborers—people who do physical work for pay

nationality—the country a person comes from

nativists—people who believe that the interests of native-born residents should outweigh the interests of immigrants

oppression—unfair, cruel treatment of a person or group

pedestal—the base of a tall object

persecution—unfair treatment

scholar—an intelligent person who knows a certain subject very well

starvation—suffering or death caused by not having enough food

Supreme Court—the highest court of the United States

tenement—an apartment building that housed especially poorer families in cities

Index

Your Turn!

In 1890, foreign-born residents made up 15 percent of the U.S. population. Today, the number is around 14 percent of the U.S. population. That means about one in seven Americans was born in another country. Combined with their children, nearly one-third of Americans are either immigrants or the children of immigrants.

Find someone you know who was born in another country. Interview them about their immigration experience. With their permission, record the interview and create a documentary about their experiences.